Speed
to Glory

Other books in the Zonderkidz Biography Series:

Speed to Glory

the
Cullen Jones
Story

Natalie Davis Miller

ZONDERVAN.com/
AUTHORTRACKER
follow your favorite authors

ZONDERKIDZ

Speed to Glory
Copyright © 2012 by Natalie Davis Miller

This title is also available as a Zondervan ebook.

Visit www.zondervan.com/ebooks

Requests for information should be addressed to:

Zonderkidz, 5300 Patterson Ave SE, Grand Rapids, Michigan 49530

ISBN: 978-0-310-72633-3

Cover design: Kris Nelson
Interior composition: Greg Johnson/TextbookPerfect

Printed in the United States

12 13 14 15 16 17 18 /DCI/ 22 21 20 19 18 17 16 15 14 13 12 11 10 9 8 7 6 5 4 3 2 1

For my mother, Rebecca P. Davis.
When I was six and came to you with stories while you
were cooking, you never said, "Not now." You said,
"That's good—can you write me another story?"
Thank you.

Table of Contents

Chapter 1

Slip Sliding Away

Ronald Jones climbed onto his inner tube and went down the waterslide just moments before his young son, Cullen, who would be riding solo on his own tube. Before going down, he told Cullen to hang onto the inner tube when he came down the chute into the pool. Following Cullen would be his mother, Debra. The family was enjoying their vacation at Dorney Park & Wildwater Kingdom in Allentown, Pennsylvania. Cullen went down, making the kinds of joyous noises that any five-year-old would make when zooming down a slide into water. And then the sounds stopped.

"I heard Cullen go down, and then I heard his screams just get cut off." This puzzled Debra, who wouldn't know the situation until she went down the slide. What Debra didn't know was that Cullen's screams were cut off by the water engulfing her young son. It's hard to scream when you're at the bottom of the pool.

Ronald was returning his inner tube and did not see Cullen come down. Debra, who could not swim, came down the slide behind Cullen. Standing at five feet eight inches, but not a swimmer, she could barely keep her head above the water. Knowing that her son was in dire trouble, she tried to get the attention of the lifeguards. When Cullen was finally brought to the surface, he was unconscious.

"When I hit the bottom of the ride, there was this huge pool of water, and I flipped right over," recalls Cullen. He was eventually rescued by his father and given mouth-to-mouth resuscitation by one of the lifeguards.

And like any kid who had just taken the ride of his life, Cullen wanted to "do it again!" Debra, who reluctantly went on the ride in the first place, said, "You must be out of your mind!"

The near-drowning incident didn't deter Cullen. Nor did it deter his mother. After the accident, Debra Jones knew she needed to provide Cullen with the skills to protect himself so she would never again worry about her son nearly drowning. She enrolled him in swimming classes the very next week.

Cullen's brush with death occurred in 1989. Less than twenty years later, he would wear Olympic gold around his neck, and hold the world record for the 50m freestyle—in swimming! A sport that nearly claimed his life years earlier took him to the top of the world.

Cullen Jones Fast Facts

The Basics

- Date of birth: February 29, 1984 (He's a leap year baby!)
- Born in the Bronx, New York
- Grew up in Irvington, New Jersey
- Parents: Ronald and Debra Jones
- Siblings: Cullen is an only child
- Nicknames: CJ, Nova
- What his mother calls him when he is in trouble: Cullen Andrew!
- Favorite color(s): a tie between red and black
- Favorite sport (other than swimming): basketball, playing and watching
- Favorite movie: Disney's *Aladdin* (I love the genie and the idea of getting three wishes.)
- Favorite book(s): *Harry Potter,* biographies, anything about Michael Jordan and Apollo Ono. "I love to read anything about people overcoming adversity."
- Favorite book in the Bible: Proverbs
- Loves video games, especially Wii and Dance Central.
- Most influential persons: his father, Ronald Jones, Coach Ed Nessel
- Home: North Carolina
- College: North Carolina State 2002 – 2006

Cullen Jones Fast Facts

Honors and Awards

- Three time NCAA All American, 2004, 2005, 2006
- Seven ACC Championships
- Gold Medals:
  - −2009 FINA World Champs, 400m freestyle relay
  - −2008 Olympics in Beijing, China, 400m freestyle relay
  - −2007 World Championships, 400m freestyle relay
  - −2006 Pan Pacific Championships, 400m freestyle relay
  - −2006 Pan Pacific Championships, 50m freestyle
  - −2005 World University Games, 50m freestyle (record 22:17)
- ACC Swimmer of the Year and ACC Meet MVP 2006
- ESPY Best Sports Moment, 2008 Olympics, 400m freestyle relay
- Dr. Leroy Walker North Carolina Male Olympian of the Year, 2008
- World Record Holder, 400m freestyle relay, 2008 Olympics
- American Record Holder, 50m freestyle, 2009
- *Sports Illustrated* Sportsman of the Year nomination, 2010
- #1 Good Guy in Sports — the Good Man Project 2011
- The Grio's 100 History Makers in the Making of 2011

Chapter 2

Growing Up Cullen Jones

On February 29, 1984, Cullen Andrew Jones was born at the Montefiore Albert Einstein Hospital in the Bronx (then known as the Albert Einstein Hospital). Cullen was born on Leap Day, and he almost wasn't born at all. The umbilical cord wrapped around Cullen's neck and nearly strangled him. But the doctors were able to deliver him through surgery, a caesarian section. (More than twenty years later, Cullen returned to the hospital—as an Olympian guest speaker, where he got to meet the doctor who delivered him—who was quite surprised and excited to learn he had delivered an Olympian!)

Cullen Andrew Jones, who would later be called CJ by his mother, was the only child of Ronald and Debra Jones. How they met is the stuff of Hollywood romance.

Cullen's parents connected one fateful day in New York City—the largest city in the United States—with a population today of more than eight million people.

However, their chance encounter wasn't the first time they had met. Both from the Bronx, Cullen's parents had dated as teenagers but eventually drifted apart. Seven years later they happened to be walking along 6th Avenue in Manhattan when they saw one another. "I was like, wow, what are the odds?" said Debra. The rest, as they say, was history.

Born in the Bronx, Cullen and his family eventually moved to Irvington, New Jersey. He began walking around the age of one, and once he became mobile, he was always on the move. As a kid, he was never content to just sit, his mother said, a fact that remains true of him today. "Even when I go to see him, he can only sit in the house for a short while before he's ready to go and explore," Debra said.

Cullen became more inquisitive as he got older, wanting to know how things worked, and his parents quickly learned they had to be careful with household items because young Cullen was apt to take them apart to see what made them tick. Yet Debra and Ronald often indulged young Cullen's appetite to know more, and they made adventures by taking him on many excursions. "I always looked forward to the weekends because I got to spend time with my mom and dad, and they were very, very active in my life," recalls Cullen.

"He would wake me up on Saturday morning ask-

A young Cullen Jones with his father and mother, Ronald and Debra.

ing what we were going to do," his mother said. "Every weekend was an adventure."

Debra traveled for her job, and Cullen often went along. He loved traveling. Even at the age of four, he had his suitcase packed to go. It may have held only toys, but Cullen was ready.

Even as an only child, Cullen was never lonely. He lived in a two-family house. He lived with his parents on the second floor, and his grandmother and uncle lived below (Debra's mother and brother). With an uncle and grandmother just a floor away, Cullen had family nearby to keep a watchful eye on him, but in New York there was one thing dividing their family—baseball! "My mom and dad were Mets fans, but my grandmother and I were Yankees fans," said Cullen. During the Subway Series, the games played between the New York major league baseball teams, Cullen would go downstairs and watch the game with his grandmother and bang on the ceiling whenever the Yankees won. "We were a house divided," Cullen said.

In addition to baseball fun, living with extended family meant always having someone around, so there was never a reason to be bored. "It was awesome!" said Cullen. His grandmother was always there, providing snacks and companionship, sharing frequent card games. "I became quite the card shark."

Like many boys at the time, Cullen was a huge movie fan, especially of Star Wars. Even now, as an adult, Cullen has a light saber his mother gave him for Christmas when he was twenty-five. The death defying, whip-wielding, grab-my-hat Indiana Jones was another favorite movie hero. Cullen also loved comic books and Matchbox cars. But Cullen found additional fun beyond toys—often at the expense of his mother.

A self-proclaimed jokester, Cullen loved pranking his parents. But according to Debra, he and his father often joined forces to play jokes on her. One of their favorites was hide and seek. She would go through their house, calling out their names, and searching until she finally found them.

Cullen would pull lots of small pranks, but nothing

utterly ridiculous, crazy, or dangerous. His enjoyment was more along the lines of messing with his parents — like hiding the remote to the television and then denying that he knew its whereabouts. Whoopee cushions were another favorite. Yet there was one particular stunt that really stood out. When Cullen was around eleven, he decided to have a little fun with his father. "I pulled all of the medicine from the cabinet up to the front so that when he opened it, it would all fall out in front of him," laughed Cullen.

Even with parents that he considered to be strict when they needed to be, Cullen quickly points out they were "pretty cool parents." So cool, that at the tender age of eleven, they let him go out on his first "date." Of course, they went with him to chaperone.

"It was cool because I was eleven years old, and I was taking a girl out! Sure my parents were there — but at the same time, I was taking a girl out!" Even the young lady thought that it was cool that she was able to go out on a date. Where did they go? To the movies, of course — one of Cullen's favorite things to do — and to Boston Market for dinner. "I got dressed up," Cullen said. "I was ready to go."

The "pretty cool parents" scored big in Cullen's book. While they were somewhat strict and very structured with Cullen's life, they also enjoyed having fun. "I remember very fondly my parents laughing quite a bit. Whether I understood the jokes or not, they laughed a lot."

Family time for the Joneses meant watching movies together and eating out. "We watched a lot of movies," said Cullen, but not at the expense of schoolwork. Debra and Ronald took Cullen's schooling very seriously. "My parents were big into my homework, so the only time I got to do anything was when everything was done. But we watched movies all the time, and I always enjoyed it."

"We would eat on trays and watch movies during dinner," Cullen said. Watching television during meals didn't concern them. "That's how we always did it, and I enjoyed every minute."

Cullen's interest in how things work continued to grow as he did. Cullen was a techno buff, something he did alongside his father, who tinkered with and fixed computers on the side, in addition to his regular day job. His father's sense of technology led Cullen to become a self-described "gadget fiend."

When Cullen wanted to play on his father's computer, his dad had a simple answer. "The only way you're going to play on a computer is if you build your own." So at the age of eleven, with his father watching over, Cullen built his own computer. Cullen's father supervised him, but he let Cullen piece it together himself. The experience left a strong impression on Cullen, who said he could still build a PC today if he had to.

"My dad was a PC guy all the way," said Cullen. But even so, Cullen bought himself an Apple computer after he received his first big contract with Nike. "I love my Apple, but I almost felt like I was going against the grain."

Chapter 3

Splashing in the Water

Debra and Ronald Jones balanced the fun in Cullen's life with a good dose of structure and discipline. "I didn't know a life without time management and structure, which I think is awesome for me because I never had a chance to really fall into the wrong crowd."

Cullen and his family lived in what he described as "a not-so-nice neighborhood," a town with rival gangs, and the sounds of bullets were sometimes heard in the evenings. "A lot of people throw around the word *ghetto*. I lived in it. For seventeen years of my life, that's where I grew up." Even so, Cullen's parents kept him away from the rough streets by keeping him actively involved in swimming. He had school, swim practice, and time at home with family.

Cullen had been pretty carefree about the water before the near-drowning incident, but once he started swim lessons, Cullen fully discovered his true love of water. He began taking classes at age five, and by age eight he was swimming competitively.

Debra Jones would never say she knew early on Cullen would become an extraordinary swimmer. She had seen too many parents put too much pressure on their children. Yet when he was ten years old, Cullen made a pronouncement to his mother. "Mom, I think swimming is my passion." Without his parents ever pressuring him, Cullen chose his path. He told his mom, "This is who I am, this is a part of me. It's going to always be a part of me."

With a mother who stood at five-foot, eight-inches, and a father stretching out to six-feet, four-inches tall, it's no wonder Cullen grew to be six-foot-five. His father was a college basketball guard, and his mother had been a modern dancer. The inherited height and athleticism, combined with Cullen's personal drive and desire, helped send his swimming career to new depths.

While swimming was a part of Cullen, it wasn't always a part of his father. With two uncles topping out over six feet, height was a trademark for the Jones men, and Ronald Jones wanted his son to become a basketball player, as he himself had been. But this would not be the case. While Cullen enjoyed basketball, both watching and playing it for fun, it just wasn't the sport for him.

As somewhat of a consolation prize to his father for not playing basketball, Cullen played water polo instead, kind of like basketball in the water. Cullen played guard, which had been his father's position in basketball. "But

[Ronald] didn't want him playing water polo," recalled Debra. "For whatever reason, he didn't like it," Ronald supported his son by attending his water polo games in high school, yet Ronald still wasn't thrilled with Cullen swimming.

As time passed, eventually Ronald warmed to the idea of Cullen swimming—so much that he took a different approach, applying pressure on Cullen to win. Debra was reminded of kids dropping out of swimming because of their parents pressuring them with their expectations of scholarships and other things. She wanted Cullen to do what he did for himself, not for her or for her husband. Debra again counseled Ronald, reminding him that Cullen already had a coach.

"Let the coach do what he has to do," said Debra to her husband. "Let [Cullen] go—he will be better. If he wants to break a plateau, let him go talk to the coaches." The role that Debra and Ronald played was that of supporters: getting Cullen to practice, getting him to meets, getting him whatever he needed to succeed. All Cullen had to do was swim.

Chapter 4

Making the Grade

When your dad is six-feet-four-inches you had better be strategic about your rebelling, according to Cullen Jones. "I love my dad to death, but I knew that when he meant business, he meant business."

"Swimming was so important to me," Cullen said. His passion for swimming was important, yes, but even so, Cullen sometimes struggled to make the best choices when it came to his passion. It's hard to imagine a record-setting, self-disciplined, swimming star would ever rebel as a child, but Cullen had his moments.

At times, Cullen admits he slacked on his homework. Debra and Ronald had told Cullen that if he wanted to swim, he would have to keep his grades up. And while his parents remained supportive, when his grades dropped, they followed through. Debra gave him the following advice: "I'll give you an opportunity to make choices, but just know when you make these choices, you have to live with the consequences."

For Cullen the consequences meant no swimming practices, no competition, no social activities, nothing but focusing on raising his grades. The punishment devastated and depressed Cullen. "I was always motivated, and they took swimming away from me."

Debra and Ronald had set high standards, but not impossible ones. They knew what they expected of their son. His parents had no problem letting his high school know. Even though Cullen was a top swimmer on the team, his parents held their ground, and Cullen couldn't swim with the team. The lack of activity left Cullen bouncing off the walls, according to his mother. Yet he had to learn to channel his energy and get his work done. "It teaches you how to put your priorities together on things you have to do," said Debra.

Cullen's depression impacted his parents. Cullen had been so negatively affected his parents decided never to punish Cullen this way again.

Even so, peer pressures sometimes got the best of him, and Cullen would sometimes skip practice to hang out with his friends. But his parents didn't punish him for skipping. Instead, when he did poorly in the next meet, his parents would make a point by saying, "You know, you probably would have won if you had gone to practice," Cullen said.

Cullen recognized his parents had his best interests at heart. They taught him that, for every action, there's an opposite reaction. "My parents had some stuff figured out. I consider myself very blessed to have them."

Debra and Ronald held Cullen accountable. They didn't hesitate to tell it like it is. "When I didn't do well at something," Cullen said, "they asked me what I planned to do next." While still being loving, his parents showed Cullen the importance of following through and being responsible, life lessons Cullen greatly appreciates today.

Chapter 5

Like a Duck in Water

From kindergarten until fourth grade, Cullen attended The Chad School in Newark, New Jersey. He then went to the Sacred Heart of Vailsburg in Newark from fourth grade to eighth grade. Cullen was eight years old when he joined his first swim team. "It was different for me," recalls Cullen. The issue wasn't the water. It was the skimpy, brief-like swimsuit the boys had to wear. "You had to walk out in front of people in this little swim suit, so yeah, it was a little rough," Cullen said. What helped Cullen was the fact that his teammates were wearing the same thing. The embarrassment didn't last long, and Cullen posted his first win when he was just eight years old in a meet against his own team.

When Cullen was ten, his best friend and co-swimmer on the team invited Cullen and his family to the Fountain Baptist Church in New Jersey. Prior to that, the Jones family had been attending a Catholic church, but it was a different experience from the previous church in New York, and Debra had not felt "at home."

However, that day, Debra and Ronald shared a "God moment." While sitting in their pew at Fountain Baptist, Debra began thinking how she wanted to go up for the alter call and join the church, and while she was sitting there thinking those thoughts, Ronald stood and said, "All right, both of you, get up. Let's go. We're joining."

From that day, Cullen attended church every weekend, connecting with the youth ministry. He became part of a new church family, in addition to his "swim team" family. Cullen's parents were big influencers in his religious beliefs. "My family was very close, so where they went, I went," said Cullen.

At age eleven, Cullen took home his first swimming ribbon. "I remember another time when I was eleven, there was this swimmer my age who had been beating me," Cullen said. "I was raised to be competitive, and when I told my mom about it, she told me I would have to try hard and listen to my coach, and eat my vegetables! I could see hard work and listening to your coach, but *vegetables*?" (Perhaps this was her way of sneaking some healthy food into his diet.)

Throughout his childhood, Cullen swam on a number of different teams and had a number of different coaches, but when he graduated from middle school, Cullen found himself without a coach. He had been swimming in the USS swimming league (now known as USA Swimming) since he was eight years old, and at fourteen he wanted to swim USS with the goal of going to the Junior Olympics. "I loved swimming in the meets and wanted to keep competing like I'd been doing." But the increased training and practices made it harder for him to attend youth group, and without a team, Cullen seriously considered quitting swimming.

At the time, entering high school, he had the choice of playing basketball or he could also swim for his high school, something Cullen wasn't used to. In a life-changing decision, Cullen chose to stick with his goals and participate in the sport that would make all the difference. "I chose swimming."

A Day in the Life of a High School Swimmer

Monday through Friday:
Morning practice: 6:00 – 7:30 a.m.
After-school practice: 3:30 – 6:00 p.m.

Saturday:
One-time practice: three-four hours

Season:
Competitive season: 15 weeks
Swim clubs: 25–30 weeks
Swimming in High School

Jess Preston

Head swim coach, Penn High School, Granger, Indiana

How to make the team:

Get to practice and have a good practice, work hard, be respectful.

Age children should start swimming:

It's never too early, and it's never too late. Some of our best swimmers started in high school. Others have been swimming since they were six or seven.

What makes an Olympian:

Sacrifice, dedication, and hard work. Putting in the time and working hard for it. Some people say it takes a lot of natural ability. Some coaches may say you have to be extremely talented. I'm more a believer in a strong work ethic.

Advice to young swimmers:

Have the willingness to work very hard, keep a positive attitude, and listen to your coaches. I think it boils down to hard work, if you are willing to put the time in. The best part about swimming is it's not always about who wins, because you can set personal goals. You don't have to be an Olympic gold medalist to be successful in this sport. Let's say your best time in the fifty-freestyle is thirty seconds. Well, your goal now is to break thirty seconds. The first time you break thirty seconds, that may not be fast to some people on your team, but that's a great feeling, a great accomplishment, because you've achieved your goal, breaking 30 seconds. So in essence, you've won by meeting your goal. You may have gotten last place in the race, but you got your best time. That's what I love about the sport. Everybody can set their own personal goals and strive for those.

Chapter 6

The Mad Stork

Cullen was happy with his decision, but in order to compete at the same level and quality for Junior Olympics, he had to find a team within the USS swimming league. He found one through the Jewish Community Center (JCC), where, for the first time, Cullen found himself the only black member of the swim team. "It was really hard for me because I didn't relate at the time," Cullen said. His earlier teams had been a mix of races. "But at the JCC, where I was the only African American, it was a hard, hard thing for me to get used to for that first year. It was my first real taste of what it meant to compete at a new level. The competition started to trickle off." On that particular team, at that particular time, "I was going to be the only black person."

Cullen's coach at the JCC was Ed Nessel, also known as Coach N. After having coached swimmers for forty-six years, today Nessel lives in Florida and works with NASA engineers and rescuers for the Navy, Coast Guard, and the Air Force. But to a young Cullen and the other swimmers, he was Coach N.

Nessel describes his first impression of Cullen as being "the mad stork." He saw Cullen, or Jonesy, as he liked to call him, as a "real string bean." He was six-feet, two-inches tall at age thirteen. Nessel described Cullen as "coachable," and said his positive attitude helped him learn to be a better swimmer. "He always had a big smile," Coach N said. "All teeth."

Cullen's strong point was that he loved to compete and be a super achiever. "He was a good kid, he was honest. He didn't do anything to get himself in trouble. Because I think his father would have killed him," joked Nessel. Ronald took a hard line with Cullen and his training. Yet, he was always there, even during the last days of his illness. "Practices started at 6:00 a.m., and his father would be there for two hours a day, six days a week."

Initially, Cullen's father didn't trust Coach N. "I had to win him over," said Nessel. "It wasn't my job, but I'm glad I did. It wouldn't have changed one bit of me working with Cullen."

Nessel knew Cullen was somewhat of an attraction—something many of the families and swimmers at the JCC hadn't seen before—a black swimmer in the pool. "Especially not a black swimmer who was so much faster than the other kids. He was that much faster."

Photo courtesy of Ed Nessel

Cullen was selected as the New Jersey Athlete of the Month in January of his senior year. Here he is arm-in-arm with Coach N., Ed Nessel.

Racism and Swimming

Did you know that there was a time when African Americans could not swim in public pools? Swimming pools and many other facilities were segregated. In some cities African Americans could only swim on the day that the pool was drained and cleaned.

Historically, more African Americans didn't know how to swim, and one major reason was because of inadequate access to swimming pools.

Municipal (city) swimming pools in America started out as public baths in the late 1800s. The first municipal pools were called swimming baths and were often frequented by the lower working class as a means for cleaning themselves. Men and women used the baths separately, and boys used the baths more frequently

(continued)

than any other group, mainly to play. Swimming was already a popular activity in local lakes and rivers.

Many young boys and men swam nude, which definitely did not appeal to the Victorian sense of decency at the time. Municipal pools were built with the hope that middle class rules would settle down the roughhouse nature of the lower class young men.

Pools were often located in immigrant, lower-class neighborhoods. During this time period, class differences were more important than race differences, and blacks and whites often bathed together.

Pools began charging entrance fees when civility and acting properly could not be enforced on the rowdy lower classes. They became places for middle and upper class men to swim, since the lower classes could not afford the fee.

The cholera epidemic and the end of the Civil War hastened the building of public baths. Cholera was thought to be spread by the uncleanliness of the poor. By the 1890s, however, the germ theory was widely believed. Microbes that survived longer in water were the cause of many diseases. Pools as bathing places changed, and cities began building public shower facilities. Showers were added to pools and pools became places for physical activity and athleticism.

"Large, leisure-resort pools" were built in the 1920s and '30s. The federal government, as part of the New Deal, built many of the pools in an effort to give jobs to Americans. The popularity of pools also increased with the use of chlorine to fight off communicable diseases. The one-piece swimsuit for women also helped to increase the number of swimmers. Women were no longer swimming in heavy, cumbersome swimsuits. Eventually, men and women would be allowed to swim together.

During this time, many pools in the north became segregated, and cities built most of their pools in white neighborhoods, limiting blacks to fewer pools. Blacks were often kept from entering pools that were predominantly white, and if they did have access to a pool, it was often a much smaller one.

When pools were built in black neighborhoods, they were often "mini pools," measuring 20 x 40 feet. The pools were so crowded that very little swimming could actually take place. When larger pools were built, they were made of concrete, surrounded by concrete, lacking trees, sand, and other pleasing features.

By the 1940s and '50s, pools were being desegregated, but whites and blacks rarely swam together. The '60s saw private, white-only pools in clubs and in homes being built, and it would take court cases against these clubs before they allowed blacks.

In the '70s, many pools suffered from decay and lack of upkeep. Local government, suffering financially, decided not to put the money into the upkeep of the current pools, or into building new pools. As the pools deteriorated, so did the attendance. Municipal pools closed without new pools to take their place. As a result, many were left without a way to learn to swim, especially African Americans.

Today's youth have many swimming options. By working with learn-to-swim providers, Cullen Jones is trying to change history and teach minorities swimming basics through his *Make a Splash with Cullen Jones* initiative.

"One time Cullen was in a meet in north Jersey, a long ride to an upscale area in Bergen County." Cullen had been nervous and lost his focus. "It was during the individual medley, and Cullen should have started with the butterfly, but he dove in and started swimming freestyle. Of course, Cullen knew he had blown it. Instant disqualification. We joke about it today."

People definitely noticed Cullen's mistake that day, Nessel said. If Cullen stumbled on the deck, people would notice. They looked at everything he did. But during that same meet, Cullen was able to rise above it all and post a good time in the 50m freestyle. "That was the fastest listed time in New Jersey the whole year. And everybody was looking at their watches. They wanted to make sure their watches weren't broken. He rose above the mistake he made earlier and laughed at himself. He handled it well."

Cullen dealt with jealousy and rudeness from other swimmers on many occasions. During one New Jersey state championship, Cullen found himself competing against another extremely fast swimmer who also happened to be black. Cullen won. As Cullen had learned from Coach N., who always enforced good manners and sportsmanship, Cullen went to shake the other swimmer's hand. "When you win, you simply say thank you when you are congratulated," Nessel said. "No big head allowed, because next week somebody else will kick your butt. Just thank God for a good swim, a good day, and simply say thank you. If you lose to somebody, extend your hand over and congratulate them. Good sportsmanship," said Nessel.

"Well this other young black swimmer, Jonesy beat him in the 50m and the 100m freestyle, and went very fast. Very good for a New Jersey swimmer. And the other kid wouldn't shake his hand." The incident may have gone unnoticed if it weren't for one small detail. "It's not hard to spot two black families in all those white people sitting there," Nessel said. "You can't hide."

Later that day, during the same event, Cullen and this swimmer competed again, and that time Cullen lost. "Mrs. Jones, being the lovely lady that she is, congratulated the other mother when her son just nipped Cullen in the 100m butterfly," Nessel said.

Nessel wanted to see Cullen and his other swimmers win with grace and lose with dignity. He didn't want them to blame anyone or to put a spin on what happened. He wanted them to be honest and true sportsmen and women. "Jonesy was never a sore loser. He would pout, just like any other normal response, but he was never a sore loser. I told him to always think before you say something, so you don't sound like a fool. He speaks pretty well, and I'm impressed with him," said Nessel.

Swimming – The Strokes

- Freestyle: Swimmer can swim any stroke; most commonly used is the crawl: an alternating stroking of the arms over the surface of the water and an alternating up and down flutter kick.
- Backstroke: An alternating motion of the arms with a flutter kick on the back. On turns, the swimmer may rotate to the stomach and perform a flip turn. Some part of the swimmer must touch the wall. The swimmer finishes on his back.
- Breaststroke: Requires simultaneous movement of the arms on the same horizontal plane. The kick is a simultaneous, somewhat circular motion similar to the action of a frog.
- Butterfly: Combines a simultaneous recovery of the arms over the water with an undulating dolphin kick.
- Medley: Swimming race, involving individual swimmers or a relay team.
- Individual Medley: Features all four strokes in the order of butterfly, backstroke, breaststroke, and freestyle.
- Freestyle Medley: Four freestyle swimmers, each swimming a quarter of the total distance of the race.
- Medley Relay: Features all four strokes in the order of backstroke, breaststroke, butterfly, and freestyle.

Cullen was never, ever treated differently or discriminated against by the swimmers on his team. If there were ever any issues, they came from parents who expressed their frustration at their child not being put into a relay, or Cullen swimming faster. Cullen heard the frustration of the parents when he started winning. He heard taunts and jeers, questions about why he was there and not playing some other sport. In an interview with *Access Hollywood*, Cullen recalled the advice his mother gave him— "Don't let anybody make you feel like less than a person. You belong here, beating their kids. You've

Greg Baker/AP Images

Cullen gets a hug from his mom after winning the gold medal at the 2008 Olympic Games. He and his mother have always had a special relationship and remain very close.

trained harder than anyone else here, so go out there and show what you've done."

One time Cullen *was* slighted, and the memory sticks with Nessel. "Cullen won all kinds of things. They had a marquee [outside the JCC] and they put little things out there — we have the best this or that. They never put his name down. To this day, that bothers me," said Nessel.

This didn't deter Cullen, who continued to compete. Yet Cullen didn't always receive a gold medal or a blue ribbon, a fact that he is quick to point out. "A lot of times when I was younger, I got the pink ribbon, which was seventh place. So I wasn't always a child prodigy. It was a huge culmination of a lot of different coaching, a lot of different coaches, watching myself swim, and watching other people swim."

Cullen didn't really start to know the feeling of winning until his later teens. He had been swimming competitively for eight years. He stayed the course and it began to pay off in greater victories.

Around this time, Cullen got his first job. He was, after all, a teenager, and Cullen wanted to look good. If a clothing gene existed, Cullen inherited it from his father. "My dad was really big into being fashionable," Cullen said. He particularly remembers a red velvet jacket his father loved to wear. "My mom was also really into looking good, and both my parents always said to me, 'When you leave the house, you're representing the Jones family. So I was never able to go outside without my hair combed and my teeth brushed."

This sense of fashion influenced Cullen as a young man, and he has a dream of someday becoming a fashion designer. "I figured out then how much I loved clothes, once I started buying them myself."

Cullen also learned something else about the fashion industry—it required money to buy those clothes he loved. In the past if Cullen wanted something from his parents, he heard two familiar words: maybe and no. "Those were the two words that I heard the most. Maybe, no, no, no, no. The only way that I got what I wanted was when I worked for it. So at the age of fifteen, I got a job."

Nessel continued to be an influence in Cullen's life, training him throughout his teen years, and Cullen would check in with Nessel during college. Nessel left Cullen with a wealth of knowledge for winning in the water and ways to prepare himself before leaving the block, such as focusing on controlling his breathing. Nessel suggested a ritual of rubbing his hands, controlling his breathing—things that would help a swimmer to control anxiety. Anxiety was often expressed in rapid shallow breathing—holding the breath, explained Nessel. This would not allow for good air exchange. "I teach them to do just the opposite—to deal with the anxiety head on, and we dealt with physiology, whether they understood it or not. They listened to me enough to do what I told them."

Nessel recalls one instance in Cullen's career when he moved away from Nessel's ritual for warming up and relieving anxiety. In 2006 Cullen raced against the World Champion Roland Schoeman. A South African, he was in America training for the Pan Pacific Championships. Schoeman and Cullen both competed in the 50m freestyle, a race that Nessel said happens very fast, with no room for mistakes.

In their meeting, Cullen introduced himself to Schoeman. According to Nessel, Schoeman responded to Cullen by saying, "Cullen who?"

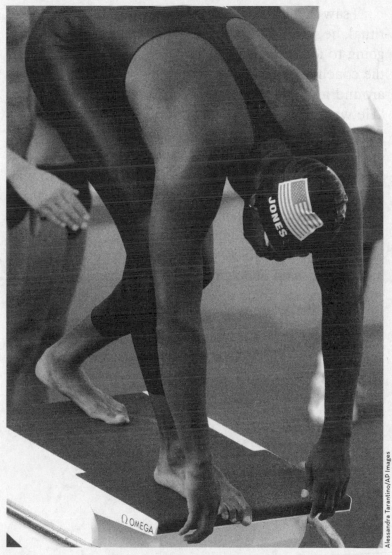

Alessandra Tarantino/AP Images

Cullen prepares to dive during a training session at the FINA Swimming World Championships in Rome, 2009. He ended up winning gold and setting yet another record with his 4x100 freestyle team.

"I saw that it bothered Jonesy, and instead of doing my ritual, he starts walking around in circles. I'm afraid he's going to lose, he's losing his focus," recalls Nessel. But the coach noticed something else—Cullen came back around and went through his routine before the race. "He went back to the way we trained, and I said, 'He's going to win it.'" Even though Schoeman was ahead at one point, Cullen pulled it out and won. Being the good sportsman he was raised to be by his parents, and thanks to the encouragement he received from Coach N. Cullen extended his hand to congratulate his rival. At least that was what Nessel thought was happening. "But I found out later he said to Schoeman, 'The name is Jones, remember it.' And Schoeman never beat him again. That smile lasted me about a year."

Growing Up a Competitive Swimmer

Craig Fox

Senior head coach
Michiana Stingrays, YMCA
South Bend, Indiana

Being on a team:

A team doesn't belong to the coaches, it belongs to the swimmers. Coaches give swimmers ownership of the team, which puts their own destiny into their own hands. We'll be here to give you the guidance, the things that you need to succeed. But ultimately, you own this program and we'll do whatever we can to meet your expectations and goals for your team.

How to make the team:

I have one requirement and it's not necessarily a swimming requirement. It's simply a willingness to be a part of what we call our Stingray Family. The one thing that we really need is acknowledgment that, okay, I'm a member of this team. I'm a member of this family. I'm a brother or sister here, and I need to be a good brother or sister. I need to be a good family member, so it's really to show that you can cooperate and work with the rest of the teammates.

Age kids should start swimming:

The sooner a child gets in the pool, the sooner he or she feels more comfortable.

What makes an Olympian:

"If your goal is to make an Olympic team, there is going to be a serious time commitment. Someone who has Olympic aspirations is going to practice twice a day, in the morning and after school, on the weekends, up to twelve practices a week. The time commitment is enormous. It's a serious challenge."

Chapter 7

Loss of an Anchor

At age sixteen, Cullen's world was rocked with the death of his father, Ronald Jones.

The family had already endured and survived two cancer scares—Cullen's grandmother was a cancer survivor, and Debra had just waged her own battle with breast cancer. She was first diagnosed in August of 1999. She had her last treatment for the cancer in January of 2000, only to have Ronald diagnosed with lung cancer on February 16, 2000.

The next day, Ronald Jones spent his birthday at his first chemo treatment for cancer. Debra had to try to keep Cullen upbeat while managing his demanding schedule of meets and practices. She also had to see to it that Ronald received his treatments.

"We knew it would be a trial in our lives, but we felt very optimistic that we would get through it together," recalled Cullen. Even when he was sick and going through chemo, his father went to every swim workout. "He showed more support for me those months than some parents show in years," said Cullen.

Through all of this, Debra and Ronald managed to keep Cullen on track with his swimming, and the family relied on the help of Coach Nessel and other friends to make sure that Cullen made practices and meets. Cullen was swimming and playing water polo for his high school, the JCC, and for USA Swimming at the time. Some of his competitions required overnight stays. Even though he swam seven days a week, Cullen was able to attend morning church services on Sunday, with Debra driving Ronald into New York for his treatments. It was a balancing act for the family.

Ronald maintained his health as long as he could, enjoying a final family vacation in August of that year in the Virgin Islands. It was then that they began to notice the toll the disease was slowly taking on Ronald's body. Often Ronald insisted that Cullen and Debra go out to dinner when he didn't feel up for it. The three would often dine in their room.

After the Labor Day holiday, the family received more disheartening news: the cancer had spread to Ronald's bones and brain. "September seventh, I watched my dad leave the house to go for a visit to the hospital—a routine visit. He returned in a wheelchair. A doctor told him that he had a few weeks to live. I watched my vibrant dad, who never missed a practice, begin to give up and ultimately pass away on November 12."

Looking back on his father's death, Cullen said it was a time of testing, especially his faith. "I asked, Why God? Why me? But my mom told me there is a reason for everything, even if we don't know why."

During that time, Cullen said very little about the death of his father to either his coach or his mother, other than pointing out that they both "saw, but didn't see." Debra explained that after Ronald's death, they finally came to terms with the fact that they had watched his slow deterioration. Debra spoke with experts in the field of cancer about what to do and say to her young son about his father's death. She was told that everybody grieves differently, and when the person was ready to talk about the death, he would. That time for Cullen didn't come until 2005.

Debra would often talk about Ronald with Cullen, regardless of whether he responded or not. She would remind Cullen that his father wasn't far from him, always looking down on him. Cullen already had been working as a lifeguard, and after his father passed away, Cullen got two more jobs so he would be able to buy things for himself and also help out his mother, who was now the sole provider for her family. Cullen never wanted to ask his mother for money. "My dad had just passed and I was sixteen and I know that she was taking a lot of the financial burden, and I never wanted to ask her for money," said Cullen.

Initially Cullen had done chores around the house and washed cars for money here and there, but at fifteen Cullen worked at the Connection for Women and

Family, a facility similar to a YMCA. The job gave him a chance to use his God-given talent and skills. "I was teaching kids how to swim and I was lifeguarding. So as soon as I could get a job, I did."

Cullen also served as a lifeguard at his high school for an hour and a half in the mornings before school started. "The teachers would come in early, and they would swim laps, so I would open the pool while they swam, and then I would go to school." He then got a job helping to maintain and care for pools.

Cullen would drive from neighborhood pool to neighborhood pool in northern New Jersey with a checklist. He would catalog everything that the pool needed (such as lifeguard buoys, etc.), looking for items that the lifeguards may have missed. He would then stock the pools with the items they needed.

Cullen's days were immersed in swimming, training, competing, teaching, lifeguarding, and maintaining pools. He worked those three jobs for a year. But that would change when he went to college.

Chapter 8

The College Lapse

Cullen's swimming ability took him to college on scholarships. "I like to believe that my steps are ordered," said Cullen. "When I was in high school, I believe God helped me decide which college was right for me, one that my mother would be comfortable with me attending, even though I was going to have to leave her in New Jersey." After putting his trust in God, Cullen found his future in swimming waiting for him at North Carolina State.

While at NCS, Cullen majored in English and minored in psychology. Swimming became a different game, and a scholarship meant he was swimming with a purpose. He was swimming for someone other than himself. He was swimming for his school. There was now an expectation of winning and excellence. His mother sat him down and explained the importance of what he was doing.

She told him how much she appreciated him getting the scholarship because his dad wasn't there, and she was doing all she could financially. She told him to do his best and think of his swimming like it was a paid-for performance. "It's no different than when you get into the corporate world. If you're performance is great, then you get paid a little more." She didn't sugar coat anything for him.

"Swimming isn't like football and basketball," Debra explained to Cullen, "sports with a strong following and plenty of scholarship money to go around." Debra's dose of reality laid a foundation for Cullen's college success.

Cullen had worked hard during his high school years — at his swimming and at part-time jobs. This made it particularly difficult for him to ask for help while he was in college. "When you go to college and you swim, or do any kind of activity, there's really no time to have a job," Cullen said. Cullen's day consisted of swimming in the morning, attending classes, swimming again, then study hall. His evening would wrap up around 8:30 or 9:00, too late to hold down a job as well. "I had to call my mom and ask her for money. She was so nice about it, but it killed me to ask."

While summers gave Cullen an opportunity to work and make money, his college years were spent mainly in training. During his sophomore year, Cullen won the 100m freestyle and the 50m freestyle in his conference, the Appalachian Athletic Conference (AAC), shocking the conference officials. All in all, Cullen won five ACC

Jason Reed/Reuters/Landov

The U.S. men's 4x100m freestyle relay team is pictured at their medal ceremony at the Pan Pacific 2006 swimming championships, 2006. The team set a new world record in the event. From left to right are Jason Lezak, Cullen Jones, Neil Walker, and Michael Phelps.

championship titles and an NCAA championship. His NCAA win in the 50m freestyle gave his college their first national swimming victory in thirteen years.

In the 2006 Pan Pacific Championship games, Cullen made history when he set a new world record in the 50m freestyle with a time of 21.84 seconds. Not only did he place first and take home a gold medal in that category, Cullen competed as part of the U.S. men's 4×100m freestyle relay team, and helped lead his team to victory, earning another gold medal alongside Jason Lezak, Neil

Walker, and Michael Phelps. He became the first African American to break a world record in the 4×100m relay.

While Cullen had great success during his college years, it came with a price. "I hurt my shoulder my junior year from overuse," said Cullen. He had been putting in hours of training, weight training, and he was swimming breaststroke, a stroke he didn't normally swim. He pulled hard off the wall and felt his shoulder shift. "Pain just shot through my arm," said Cullen. "They rehabbed my shoulder for weeks."

The shoulder injury occurred right before his team's conference championship, and Cullen decided to swim through the pain despite the injury. The way he saw it, he had two choices: not swim and let the team down, or grit his teeth and swim anyways. He swam, and his team won.

Another injury occurred during Cullen's senior year during a weight-lifting exercise, which took a lot longer to rehab and gave Cullen another setback. Still, most importantly, Cullen didn't give up.

Swimming in College

Ray Looze

Coach, Swimming and Diving
Indiana University

Why swimming is tough:

I think outside of boxing, it's probably the hardest sport in the world. Why? The time commitment, the energy that it takes, the dedication, and you have to train hard to be good at this sport. That means you really have to push yourself. It's painful. It's not for the weak of heart. It's a sport of repetition. It takes thousands of strokes to get your technique refined.

Why you have to work so hard:

It's a sport where once you get a little success in it, you can dictate what you're going to become. You don't have to be the smartest person; you don't have to be the most athletically gifted. You decide your work ethic. If you're a hard worker, there's nothing you can't do. You have to be a hard worker to be successful at this.

Age children should start swimming:

As soon as possible. Children as young as two can learn to stay afloat.

Advice to young swimmers:

Be consistent, learn how to push yourself, be confident, be aggressive — that means, don't wait for stuff to happen — make it happen. It's like life — show up. Good things are going to happen if you're at practice.

What makes an Olympian:

There are some natural gifts that lend themselves toward being a good swimmer. We call it *feel for the water*. You're at home in the water. And then you refine that with good coaching.

On Cullen Jones:

He's a blade. He just slices through the water. It's beautiful.

Character Traits Built in the Pool

- Discipline
- Work ethic
- Goal setting
- Teamwork
- Integrity
- Leadership skills
- Ability to overcome adversity

Chapter 9

On the Olympic Road

It was during Cullen's college years when a family friend first predicted Cullen would make it in the Olympics. Still, Debra never pressured him. If Cullen was going to be in the Olympics, she didn't want him to do it for her. "I never wanted him to think he was doing it for me," said Debra. "That puts such pressure on an athlete." All along, Debra made sure Cullen did what he did for the right reasons. "Do it for yourself. Do it because you want to do it. I'm just here to support you. I'm your rah-rah group. I'm here if things don't go the way you want. I'm here to hold you and pass you the tissues."

Again, not one for sugarcoating, Debra also told Cullen if he needed a tissue, he'd have fifteen minutes — all the time she would allow for a pity party. "After that you get up and make a decision on what you need to move forward. You've spilt those tears. Let's move on."

Osman Orsal/AP Images

Cullen shakes hands with Andrey Kapralov of Russia after winning the men's 50-meter freestyle final competition during the 23rd World University Games, 2005.

As a mother looking at her son who is trying to make his way in the world, she knew that this plan of action would give him a sense of control and remove that feeling of hopelessness. "It's so easy to fall into that pity party, where you don't think you have control, and you feel overwhelmed. I wanted him to know that there is something you can do." She and Cullen would talk, but she let him figure out what to work on. She would prompt him with questions. "Do you know what may have stopped you from making your goal? You stumble, but it's not the end of the world," she would say.

In the summer of 2006, shortly after the Pan Pacific Swimming Championships, Cullen decided to pursue swimming as a professional, and in doing so, he made the tough decision to end his college career early. College had provided Cullen with a platform to express his skills and God-given talent in swimming. And of course, it provided him with a great education, but as a professional swimmer, Cullen found it difficult to pursue his college diploma while swimming professionally. "So I had to make the decision to travel, promote myself and be a great swimmer, or make the decision to finish school. At that point I was doing really well. I had just set the world record."

Before making the decision, Cullen talked it over with his mother. He was, of course, very nervous talking to Debra about dropping out of school. Debra's response was completely unexpected. "She said, 'I understand. Do what you've got to do.'"

With his mother's blessing, Cullen went pro, signing a contract with Nike that gave him two million dollars over seven years. At the time, this was the biggest endorsement for a short-distance swimmer.

Prior to his world-breaking swim at the Pan Pacific games, Cullen had competed in the 2004 Olympic trials, but he didn't qualify, mainly because Cullen psyched himself out.

Cullen was a bit daunted when 10-time Olympic medalist Gary Hall showed up wearing boxing shorts and a robe and began shadow boxing and flexing for the audience. "That's the biggest hurdle for me, how to psych myself up. I still have slip-ups," said Jones in the article.

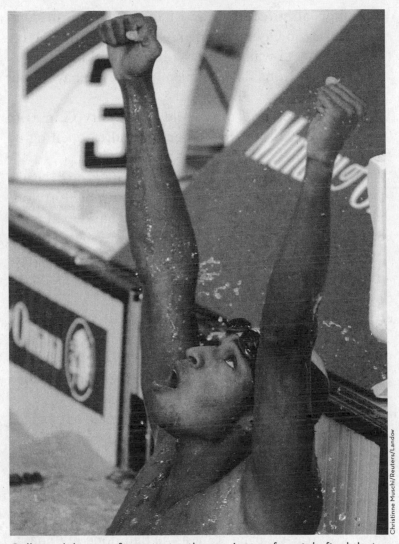

Christinne Muschi/Reuters/Landov

Cullen celebrates after winning the men's 50m freestyle final during the Pan Pacific 2006 swimming championships. This event gave Cullen the honor of becoming the first African American to break a world record in the 4x100 relay and the 50m freestyle.

Cullen admired Hall and had watched him compete in the '96 Olympics when Cullen was growing up. "That's where I want to be," Cullen had told his father.

"Really?" Ronald had replied. "Then you have to put some work in."

It took attending the World University Games in Turkey in 2005 to bring Cullen around to opening up about his father's death.

In honor of this father, Cullen got a tattoo on his back, a circle, representing the sun, with the number forty-one in its center. Forty-one was his father's basketball number. (Today, Cullen also honors his father by signing a "41" when he signs autographs.) "The cross is the sign of my faith," said Cullen. "The sun is my strength, and the Jones 41 is in remembrance of my dad."

"That was the beginning of him finally talking about my husband's death," said Debra.

Another breakthrough occurred in 2008, when Cullen was in China for the Beijing Olympics. "Cullen called me from China to say he had a dream of his father," said Debra. "And in the dream Ronald apologized to Cullen, saying he didn't want to leave, but he had to go, and he loved Cullen." Debra told Cullen she didn't know what would happen at the Olympics, but she knew it would be fantastic.

Prior to the 2008 Olympics in Beijing, Hall pulled the same costume-wearing stunt as he had done in Omaha, Nebraska, at the '04 Olympic trials. He stepped out in a floor-length cape emblazoned with "The Godfather of Swimming" on the back. When his name was announced,

Jamie Squire/Getty Images

Gary Hall Jr., left, and Cullen Jones, right, prepare for the final of the 50 meter freestyle during the 2008 U.S. Swimming Olympic Trials. Hall liked to play head games with other competitors by wearing a cape and bringing his fingers up to a six-shooter stance, mock shooting and then "blowing" off the imaginary smoke from his fingertip.

Hall brought his fingers up to a six-shooter stance, mock shooting and then "blowing" off the imaginary smoke from his fingertip.

At the time, Hall's 2008 appearance was his bid for a first ever three-peat, going for his third gold Olympic medal in the 50m freestyle. But first Hall would have to get out of the final and make the Olympic team.

Again, the over-the-top showmanship of Hall left Cullen out of sync. "The crowd ate it up," said Coach N. "It was like déjà vu. Jones beats him to the wall but didn't make the team." Cullen finished third behind Garrett Weber-Gale and Ben Wildman-Tobriner. Since only the top two advanced to compete in Beijing, Jones couldn't compete as an individual. Ironically, Cullen set an American record in the 50m freestyle preliminaries the day before, swimming 21.59, a record that eclipsed the previous record of 21.76 set by Gary Hall Jr. in 2000.

Cullen took it hard. Coach Nessel, who has worked with swimmers for forty years, said he tried to emphasize to his swimmers that the person next to them is just "another piece of bone and meat—it doesn't mean a thing," he said. "If you lose your focus, you lose."

Debra Jones recalls that Cullen was devastated about not qualifying for the individual 50m freestyle, but she quickly reminded him that he had still made the relay team. In her no-nonsense approach, she pointed out to Cullen the other athletes who had missed their opportunity by just fractions of a second. She reminded him of the possibility of greatness before him, telling him, "You at least made the team. You are now an Olympian

Cullen dives in to start his leg of the 2008 Beijing Olympics men's 4x100m freestyle relay.

because you did that. Whether you get a gold in Beijing or not, you are still an Olympian."

Even though he had lost the 50m individual trials, Cullen still competed in the 2008 Olympics as part of the 4×100m freestyle relay team, and he got that spot because he earned it—as one of the top six finishers in the 100m freestyle trials.

As a result, Cullen became part of a world-record-breaking relay team, along with Nathan Adrian, Ben Wildman-Tobriner, and Matt Grevers. In the preliminaries, Cullen was the fastest swimmer in the group, and set the record at 3:12.23.

Adrees Latif/Reuters/Landov

Garrett Weber-Gale, Jason Lezak, Michael Phelps, and Cullen Jones of the U.S. celebrate a last-second, come-from-behind win that set a world record of 3:08.24 and won the gold medal in the men's 4x100m freestyle relay.

On the eve of their competition, Cullen and the other swimmers received rock-star treatment when they were visited by members of the USA basketball team. Michael Phelps pulled Cullen from his room to meet NBA greats like LeBron James. Cullen told his mother how surprised LeBron had been when he met Cullen. "We got a brother on the team?" LeBron asked.

In the 4×100m Olympic freestyle finals, Cullen joined teammates Michael Phelps, the lead-off swimmer, Garrett Weber-Gale, and Jason Lezak. The French had been "trash talking" the Americans, promising a win. The race was tight, for sure. When Cullen swam the third leg, they were behind the French. But in a stunning come-from-behind victory, Cullen took his place in history as part of the team that would give teammate Michael Phelps his historic eighth Olympic gold medal and Cullen his first.

While television announcers were predicting a second place finish for the Americans, Jason Lezak, the anchor of the team, fought the water with every stroke to pull ahead of the Frenchman, Alain Bernard, winning by a fingertip. The Americans won the gold—and set yet another record—3:08.24. The French came in second, followed by Australia.

The phenomenal come-from-behind win was shown on television, the Internet, and eventually in print all over the world. There were shots of Phelps and Garrett Weber-Gale celebrating after Lezak touched the pad. But one member of the team was missing—Cullen Jones. Cullen didn't go far though. He went to the end of the pool to get a better look at the photo finish. When he realized they had won, he began celebrating. During his leg of the race, Cullen remained focused and intent on winning. He described himself in the moment as, "Head down, gritting my teeth, just trying to put my hand on the wall."

The rules require the swimmer to be out of the water before the next swimmer returns. Feeling a little dizzy after his race, his goal was to get out of the water and watch the end. "I was so frozen watching that race that

Mark J. Terrill/AP Images

Members of the U.S. relay team wave with gold medals during an awarding ceremony after setting a world record in the men's 4x100-meter freestyle relay final at the Beijing 2008 Olympics. They are from left: Michael Phelps, Garrett Weber-Gale, Cullen Jones, and Jason Lezak.

when [Lezak] hit, I had to run around to the other guys and try to celebrate with them," said Cullen. And the team swam like a unit. The Americans had been seen as the underdogs, but the world found out dogs run in packs.

Chapter 10

Make a Splash with Cullen Jones

After the 2008 win in the 4×100m freestyle relay, Debra reminded her son of the power he had to influence so many kids, especially African Americans. She reminded him again that it didn't matter that he hadn't qualified to compete in the 50m freestyle. She told him, "Whether you made that individual event or not didn't make any difference. They saw a black Olympian win and break a world record and be part of that team. That's all they saw."

Cullen, now an Olympian, would find his calling when USA Swimming approached him to be the face of a learn-to-swim campaign reaching out to minority communities. Make A Splash with Cullen Jones would bring the message of learning to swim to kids all across the country. The message has been about more than just teaching kids to swim with the hopes of someday being an Olympic swimmer. The message has also been about saving lives.

In August of 2010, national news reported the drowning of six teenagers in Shreveport, Louisiana. The teens were with their families at a barbeque. Initially, they were wading in knee-deep water, in an area unfamiliar to them. What they didn't know was that they were near an eighteen-foot drop off. The sand in the river gave way to a deep sinkhole. Not one of the victims, all African Americans, knew how to swim. Seven teens went under, and only one survived. The survivor was the first one to go in. The other six drowned trying to save him. He was pulled from the water by a boat. Family members, all on the riverbank, watched in horror. None of them were able to rescue any of the teens because they couldn't swim either.

"Swimming gets this reputation as kind of being the country club sport," said Sabir Muhammad, the first African American to break an American swimming record. "No one dies from not being able to play basketball." A truer statement could not have been spoken. The ability to swim is more than a physical activity or a game. It's a skill that can save countless lives every year.

"What happened in Louisiana is a tragedy," said Cullen. "My heart feels very heavy when I hear of these things." Cullen Jones knows what it feels like to nearly drown. Much like the story of the Shreveport six who drowned, his mother could not swim, and she couldn't save him. It was by the grace of God, and with the help of his father and the lifeguards, that he is alive today to tell his story. And more than just telling it, Cullen is traveling the country to share his story and a message of how important it is for children to learn how to swim, particularly minorities.

A study conducted by the University of Memphis found that fear of drowning was one reason why parents didn't encourage their children to learn to swim, even when the lessons were free. Another concern was physical appearance—of what the water would do to African American hair and skin—which for many is easily dried out and damaged by excessive use of water and chemicals. Finally, costs of swimming and limited access to pools were also contributors to the inability of minorities to swim.

These statistics and Cullen's own near-drowning experience were enough to make him want to do something about the dangerous situation affecting minorities. Cullen joined the USA Swimming Foundation and ConocoPhillips to promote water safety in their Make a Splash with Cullen Jones water safety initiative.

"Our goal is for all children in the U.S. to learn to swim, so we've created a nationwide network—partnership with swim lesson providers," said Kim O'Shea, Make a Splash program manager. According to O'Shea, the USA Swimming Foundation provides grants—money—to help pay for swim lessons for children. ConocoPhillips makes a charitable donation to the USA Swimming Foundation to help them provide free or low-cost swim lessons for children.

Kristi DesJarlais, manager for Global Brand and Community Investment, said that their relationship with the USA Swimming Foundation is "hand-in-glove,"

According to the USA Swimming Foundation 2008 statistics:

- Nine people drown each day in the United States, but in ethnically diverse communities, the drowning rate is more than double the national average.
- Nearly 70 percent of African American children and 58 percent of Hispanic children have low or no swimming ability, compared to 40 percent of their white counterparts.
- In ethnically diverse communities, the youth drowning rate is more than double the national average.
- A third of white children from non-swimming families go on to learn to swim. Less than one tenth of African American children from non-swimming families go on to learn to swim.

which is to say a perfect fit. "They have the platform to be able to spread awareness of this issue along with our help to fund this," said DesJarlais. "Safety is a core value at ConocoPhillips. We feel a responsibility to promote safe practices in our community where our employees live and work."

Make a Splash educates parents about the importance of getting their children into swim lessons through their national campaign. They also work with local learn-to-swim partners to provide water safety education in communities all around the country, and they reach diverse and underrepresented communities—those who may not have access to pools or money to pay for swimming lessons.

The program began in 2007, and over $1.8 million dollars in grants have been provided to help children learn to swim. By working with learn-to-swim providers, such as USA Swimming member clubs, local YMCAs, Boys

& Girls Clubs, parks and recreation departments, school districts, summer league programs, and learn-to-swim programs that have partnered with USA Swimming, the water safety initiative helps reduce the cost of swimming lessons. Currently, there are 492 local Make a Splash partners in 47 states, according to the USA Swimming Foundation. In the future they hope to partner with lesson providers in Montana, Wyoming, and Rhode Island, with the goal of making it to five hundred partners by the end of 2012. In just four years, the local partners have had over 1.1 million enrollments in swim lesson programs. Make a Splash has provided scholarships to pay for swimming lessons for over 38,500 of those enrollments, and local partners have come through by funding another 45,400 local enrollments.

"Many of these children would have never had the opportunity to learn to swim without these scholarships," said O'Shea. "Our local partners also host community water safety days to help spread the message of how important it is for children to learn to swim."

The Make a Splash with Cullen Jones tour makes six stops each year around the country. They have visited seventeen cities so far, including Miami, St. Louis, Chicago, Washington, D.C., New York City, Indianapolis, and Houston. Cullen has talked to 3,700 children on his tour — 3,700 children who will hopefully learn how to swim, if they don't know how to already. Cullen shares his story of how he nearly drowned and how his mother put him into swimming lessons.

Everywhere Cullen goes the media is there to take his

picture or interview him, and the word is spreading about Make a Splash. Parents and grandparents hear the drowning statistics, and they contact a provider about swim lessons for their children and grandchildren. Some people thought that one man wouldn't be able to make a difference, but Cullen is making a difference, city by city.

Make a Splash hopes to keep spreading the word about how important it is for children to learn to swim. They are working with community leaders and potential sponsors all over the country with one goal in mind: making sure that every child in the United States learns to swim. Even with adults around, as was the case with Cullen when he nearly drowned, accidents can still happen.

"Something that I don't always get to tell in my story is that day in the amusement park, I was fully supervised. So many times people think that because there are lifeguards on duty, they are completely safe from accidents," said Cullen in a CNN Health Blog posted in January 2012. "I myself was a lifeguard. When you are watching over five hundred children with your coworkers, it is not an easy task. There is a simple solution and that's swim lessons. Parents need to make it a priority for their children to learn to swim. Any body of water can be dangerous without proper instruction. Swimming is a fun activity. Learn to swim."

Chapter 11

Kids Get Wet with Make a Splash

Cullen travels all over the country talking to the children and getting in the water with them. "A lot of times I've heard parents say, 'You are an inspiration for my kid to start swimming,'" said Cullen. "I can't explain how that touches me."

Many of the children look like a young Cullen Jones, skinny, new to swimming, and a minority. "When I'm working with Make a Splash, getting kids excited about swimming, and I walk out in a brief [swimsuit] and they're just like, 'Ah ...' and I'm like, yeah, it's okay. You know it's just fun. It's fun," said Cullen, recalling the time when he was eight years old and concerned about his debut wearing the tiny swimsuit. "It was hard for me too, so I really understand where they're coming from when that shock happens. I definitely had that as a kid."

Once the initial shock wears off, the kids are at ease

Brian Lawdermilk/AP Images for USA Swimming

Cullen speaks to students during a youth assembly at Creswell Elementary School as part of the national water safety campaign *Make a Splash with Cullen Jones* which helps develop learn-to-swim programs around the country.

with Cullen and the water. Talia Mark, the manager of marketing programs at the USA Swimming Foundation, has seen Cullen in action on his tours. She describes his tour day as starting out with an early morning breakfast with community leaders, those who have influence over keeping pools open, and those who are concerned and interested in water safety lessons in their community. Breakfast is usually followed by Cullen making an appearance and talking for about thirty minutes to children at their school or group assembly. Then a few children, five to six, are selected for an in-the-water lesson with Cullen.

"Overall, the kids are timid at first, but excited to meet an Olympian," said Talia. This is to be expected— imagine meeting an Olympian, who at six-feet five-inches towers over the tallest child. "To kids he's like a giant. Just to see the kids looking up to him is something else." But big or not, Cullen brings himself down to earth by getting involved with the kids, making them feel comfortable about being in the water. Talia has traveled with Cullen, and she sees how fantastic he is with kids, even the little ones.

"One of the things that Cullen does to warm kids up is he helps them to put their swim caps on and it's just really cute because of the way that he does it. He gets the kids involved, and he puts the swim caps on so quickly. You see the kids and the parents struggling with the swim caps and he makes it a game for the kids. They really enjoy it and it gets the kids smiling and laughing," said Talia. "So from pretty much that point on, the kids are warmed up to Cullen. He's joking and laughing with them and giving them high-fives. It's really nice and a good photo op. A lot of the parents take pictures of Cullen putting caps on the kids."

Before anyone gets into the water with Cullen, all of the children are seated on the edge of the pool with their legs in the water. Cullen takes about five minutes to speak with the kids, learning each child's name, a task

Mike Derer/AP Images

Cullen talks about water safety to youngsters at the pool in
Newark, N.J., where he learned to swim.

he's quite good at according to Talia. Cullen works with
each child one-on-one in the water, but not without first
explaining safety rules and how the swim lesson will
go. Only one child is allowed in the water at a time, and
each child has to be in contact with the side of the pool.

Cullen then goes down the line asking if any of them
know how to swim. Some hands may go up, but that
changes when Cullen asks them if they took swim lessons. It's important for the children to know what it
means to really know how to swim and not just play in
water they can stand up in.

There is a general routine that Cullen follows on his tour. The kids can kick the water with their feet, and after getting in, Cullen plays games with the children. He said a familiar rhyme, "Motor boat, motor boat, go so slow," and the children kick their feet slowly. And then he said, "Motor boat, motor boat, go so fast," and they really get the water moving with their feet. "For the kids, it's getting them used to having water all over their face and shoulders. It's getting them into the water, and they don't really recognize it," said Talia.

The smaller children get to pretend that they are starfish floating on their backs with arms and legs out to the side. "He'll tell the kid that he's holding, and he'll say, 'Close your eyes,' and the kid will start to float by themselves. Or Cullen will kind of hold them up with one finger and count, one – two – three! And the kids on the side will yell, 'Wake up!' Cullen will pick the kid up and splash them in the water really quickly and then it will be the next person's turn," describes Mark. "Cullen is so good with the kids, because if they are a little nervous, he'll play games with them in the water, he'll splash them with the water and then the kids start splashing back and then it's a big game. But it's still very serious because Cullen understands that water can be a fun thing, but it's also very serious, and he explains all of that to them."

Talia recalls one tour stop in August 2011. "We were in Oklahoma City, Oklahoma, and there was this one little girl, about four years old. She could not get her swim cap on at all. She started to get really nervous because

Part of Cullen's training routine is to help the young children learn to float on their backs.

she had to get into the water, the water was cold, and she really was not trying to hear anything that Cullen had to say," recalled Talia. "But he took his time with her. He was doing the same lessons that he does at every tour stop, having the kids kick the water and having them blow bubbles in the water and having them go under the water. But for the little girl he recognized that this was going to be a completely different case for her."

Talia said that at one point the little girl got up from the side of the pool and went to her mom. Talia and others tried talking to the child, reassuring her that what she was about to do was something very big and that she was doing a great job. Cullen was also encouraging the little girl. They let her know that she could in fact do it—trust Cullen and get into the water.

Cullen took his time with the little girl, and he was eventually able to get her off the side of the wall. She let him carry her. "And then she started to smile a little bit. And then she started to laugh a little bit. And then by the end of it, she was floating on her back in the water with Cullen just holding her with his finger under her, just holding her up. That picture made it into the local newspaper," said Talia. "He's very good with kids."

If the young "swimmers" have a higher skill level, Cullen works with them on streamlining in the water, showing them how to swim and move through the water faster. Or he may work with them on perfecting a stroke they already know. He uses very few props—himself and kickboards.

Cullen's care with the children is a story heard all over the country at his many tour stops. "I don't even know if he sees it as work," said Talia. "It's a fun thing that he likes to do, but it's also changing lives of kids around the country."

Make a Splash is also reaching out to educate parents about the importance of their children learning how to swim. "Some parents are nervous because maybe they don't know how to swim, while some of them understand that this is probably going to be one of the bigger moments in their child's life. They're in the water with a gold medalist," said Talia of the children.

Parents who don't swim may be the reason why their

children don't swim, so it is important that they hear Cullen's message too. Once Cullen gets started, everyone is having fun, taking pictures, and smiling. For Cullen, it is a long day when he is on tour, but a day that is worth it, a day that could possibly save lives.

The Make a Splash initiative has been so influential in teaching children to swim that it was the recipient of the 2010 Rings of Gold award by the US Olympic Committee (USOC). According to the US Swimming Foundation, the Rings of Gold award "recognizes a program dedicated to helping children develop their Olympic or Paralympic dreams and reach their highest athletic and personal potential."

Can one person make a difference? Cullen Jones is making a difference and you can too. If you would like to see the award-winning Make a Splash program become partners with a learn-to-swim provider in your community, go to www.usaswimming.org for more information. You'll also find information about Cullen Jones, other Olympic swimmers, and how you can become an exceptional swimmer.

A History of Competitive Swimming

People have been swimming for thousands of years. Sculptures dating from 850 BC show scenes of swimmers in military battles and crossing streams. In Europe, the National Swimming Society of England held regular swimming competitions in London by 1837. But things didn't get really interesting until 1844, when The Swimming Society invited two North American Indians named Flying Gull and Tobacco to participate in a staged exhibition in London.

In England at that time, competitive swimming had become a fairly popular sport. The British generally swam the breaststroke, but Flying Gull and Tobacco moved through the waters at an incredible speed using a stroke most Europeans had never seen. Observers said, "They thrashed the water violently with their arms, like sails of a windmill, and beat downward with their feet, blowing with force and forming grotesque antics."

What they were watching is now known as the crawl. This form of swimming didn't "take" among the British, and they continued their breaststroke. But the crawl, or versions of it, had actually been used centuries earlier in the Americas, West Africa, and some Pacific islands.

By 1880, more pools were being built, and swimming had become so popular that the Amateur Swimming Association of Great Britain was established. Around this time, J. Arthur Trudgen, on a trip to South America, noticed the natives moving through the water with great speed while using an overhand stroke. When Trudgen returned to England, he began teaching what would be called the Trudgen stroke.

Another countryman, Frederick Cavill, also noted a swim technique being used by natives of the South Seas islands that involved a different kick. Cavill returned home and began teaching this new swim form, much like the freestyle form used by Charles M. Daniels in the 1910 Olympics. The stroke became known as the American crawl, and Daniels, an American, won four gold medals.

Duke Kahanamoku of Hawaii also used the crawl, or freestyle stroke, and won the 100m Olympic races in 1912 and 1920. He had learned the crawl as a child by watching the older natives of his home island. He said this stroke was used by many generations of his people.

In 1924, American Johnny Weissmuller took the world by storm when he won the 100m race at the Paris Olympic Games and defeated Kahanamoku. Weissmuller went on to win race after race, including two gold medals at the 1928 Amsterdam Olympics. He won races from 50 yards to 880 yards, grabbing five Olympic gold medals, setting world records in sixty-seven different events, while holding fifty-two national titles. He became hugely successful when he went from the swimming pool to the silver screen in Hollywood, where he starred in the movie adaptations of Edgar Rice Burroughs' books about Tarzan, the ape-man.

Other strokes have changed and developed over the years. The breaststroke was swum with the head out of the water. The backstroke was introduced during the 1900 Olympics, and the butterfly appeared in 1956. From generation to generation, through science, skill, and determination, swimmers continue to get faster and faster.

Chapter 12

Life in the Fast Lane

The IUPUI Natatorium in Indianapolis, Indiana, is described as one of the world's fastest pools. Built in 1982, it has brought success to many swimmers, including Cullen Jones, who set the American record in the 50m freestyle there in 2009. In March 2012, Cullen returned to the "Nat" for the Indy Grand Prix, the fifth stop in a seven-stop series. He was joined by other swimming greats such as Michael Phelps, Ryan Lochte, Garrett Weber-Gale, Dana Vollmer, Allison Schmitt, and Missy Franklin, just to name a few. With hundreds of men and women competing at the event, it provided the high-impact competition that would help prep Cullen for the Olympic Team trials in Omaha, Nebraska in June 2012.

"I love this pool," said Cullen of the Nat. "This is definitely a pool I've had a lot of success in. I made a couple of teams—my first team ever I made in this pool.

In 2005 I made the World University team. I got first in the 50m freestyle. I made my first international meet in this pool, so it's got some serious ties to me."

Preparing for the Olympic trials involves more than just swimming. There are many competitions; most of them away from home. Sometimes the road can take a lot out of an athlete.

"The road is challenging," said Cullen. "From trying to make sure that you eat the right things to just being away from home and being away from your bed. Just being normal, still going to practice and training, but having to do it at different pools, it gets kind of challenging for me."

In addition to traveling for swim meets, Cullen also hits the road to take his learn-to-swim message through Make A Splash to kids all over the country. "My biggest trial has been trying to make sure that I get the workouts in, getting everything together, on top of being exhausted and tired from talking to 1200 kids. It is very draining, from doing that to hopping in the pool and physically exhausting yourself some more. It's been tough, but I think I've made it work."

Cullen trains with SwimMac in Charlotte, North Carolina. The team is comprised of fifteen professional swimmers. As a professional, a swimmer competes for money. The prize money varies from meet to meet, and depending on the number of first place finishes, a swimmer can earn points, leading to more money. In addition to the financial gain, winners are sometimes awarded a medal or some other token. Cullen has a sponsor—

Nike. With a salary, Cullen is expected to perform. "I train, and I have to get to a certain level every year or else I get a pay cut. So it's a lot like any other sport," explains Cullen of the income that comes from endorsements.

David Marsh, CEO and Director of Coaching at SwimMac, is Cullen's coach. He is hard-pressed to cite a weakness in Cullen, with the exception of the competing interests for Cullen's time. "Cullen has other pulls from his successful business of doing speaking [engagements] and clinics and things like that. When he does that, he gives his all," said Marsh. "He'll stay and sign every autograph. He doesn't stay for one hour; he'll stay for three hours. He'll get in the water with the kids. He'll go above and beyond and I think to some degree, in terms of training from a pure coaching standpoint, that can be a challenge for him."

Marsh doesn't hesitate to list Cullen's strengths as he prepares for the Olympic trials, and ultimately the 2012 London Olympics. He has worked with Cullen over the last four years. "His strength as a swimmer is that he is a beautiful aquatic athlete. When he's in the water, he's very natural. His body position in the water, his ability to establish a big catch in the water when he's doing his powerful strokes — there is certainly a gift element that he's been given."

Cullen is training in the 50m freestyle, the 100m freestyle, and possibly the 4×100m freestyle relay and the 4×100m medley, which he should also freestyle in. "I have four possibilities — possible events that I can score and do well in."

The average day for Cullen is anything but average. "We do a lot of cross training—tons of cross training," said Cullen. "My coach's big thing is to be fit and be athletic." Being athletic may mean figuring out how to dunk a basketball—backwards.

Basketball is just another activity the swimmers do out of the water. They have a number of fun, athletic activities to do that proves that they aren't just fish out of the water—they are land-based mammals too. They climb ropes, which correlates to swimming with the pulling motion. They run, play ultimate Frisbee, basketball—anything that correlates to swimming and being athletic. "It keeps me very entertained during practice," said Cullen.

Swim practices are usually planned events lasting between two-and-a-half to three hours, but the coach may decide they need to work on something not previously planned. Mondays and Thursdays are usually double practices while Tuesdays, Wednesdays, Fridays, and Saturdays are single practices. All of this prepares the elite swimmers for competition throughout the year and ultimately for the Olympics.

Interestingly enough, Marsh echoes what Coach Ed Nessel had to say about Cullen—that he is very coachable. "He's been willing to accept stroke changes and detail changes through the four years I've had him," said Marsh. Again, like Nessel, Marsh sees just how competitive Cullen can be. "As the event gets bigger, as the competition gets better, as the lights get brighter, he gets better."

From left, Garrett Weber-Gale, Michael Phelps, and Cullen Jones accept their ESPYs for the best moment award for setting a world record in the men's 4x100-meter freestyle relay and winning gold at the Olympics.

As time winds down to the next Olympics, Cullen has progressively improved in the pool. "I think he's learned a lot," said Marsh. "And he is a much more mature swimmer, as to when he needs to press, when he can back off a little bit, and when he can push himself. As swimmers get older, they can't just put the hammer down all the time. They have to do some recovery."

With the 2012 Olympic games approaching, the field of fast swimmers has grown. Yet one will stand apart, not necessarily for the times he pulls down in the water, but for the differences he makes in the lives of others. "Cullen is a great role model for young kids," said Marsh. "He's not just one of those guys that's best in the world at what he does. Cullen *is* best for the world. He is that kind of guy."

Swimming Terms – Abridged

Anchor—the final swimmer in a relay. Also a term coaches use for the beginning of all four strokes indicating the "high elbow," "catch," or "early vertical forearm."

Backstroke—one of the four competitive racing strokes, basically any style of swimming on your back. Backstroke is swum as the first stroke in the Medley Relay and second stroke in the IM. Racing distances are 50 yards/meter, 100 yards/meter, and 200 yards/meter (LSCs with 8-under divisions offer the 25 yd back).

Blocks—the starting platforms located behind each lane. Minimum water depth for use of starting blocks is four feet. Blocks have a variety of designs and can be permanent or removable.

Breaststroke—one of the four competitive racing strokes. Breaststroke is swum as the second stroke in the Medley Relay and the third stroke in the IM. Racing distances are 50 yards/ meter, 100 yards/meter, and 200 yards/meter. (LSCs with 8-under divisions offer the 25 yd breast).

Butterfly—one of the four competitive racing strokes. Butterfly (nicknamed "fly") is swum as the third stroke in the Medley Relay and first stroke in the IM. Racing distances are 50 yards/meter, 100 yards/meter, and 200 yards/meter (LSCs with 8-under divisions offer the 25 yard fly).

Championship Meet—the meet held at the end of a season. Qualification times are usually necessary to enter meet.

Championship Finals—the top six or eight swimmers (depending on the number of pool lanes) in a prelims/finals meet who, after the prelims are swum, qualify to return to the finals. The fastest heat of finals when multiple heats are held.

Closed Competition—swim meet which is only open to the members of an organization or group. Summer club swim meets are considered to be "closed competition."

Club—a registered swim team that is a dues-paying member of USA-S and the local LCS.

Code of Conduct—a code of conduct that both swimmers and coaches are required to sign at certain USA-S/LSC-sponsored events. The code is not strict and involves common sense and proper behavior.

Course—designated distance (length of pool) for swimming competition (i.e., long course = 50 meters, short course = 25 yards or 15 meters).

Deadline—the date meet entries must be "postmarked" by to be accepted by the meet host. Making the meet deadline does not guarantee acceptance into a meet since many meets are "full" weeks before the entry deadline.

Deck—the area around the swimming pool reserved for swimmers, officials, and coaches. No one but an "authorized" USA Swimming member may be on the deck during a swim competition.

Dehydration—the abnormal depletion of body fluids (water). The most common cause of swimmers' cramps and sick feelings.

Distance—how far a swimmer swims. Distances for short course are: 25 yards (1 length), 50 yards (2 lengths), 100 yards (4 lengths), 200 yards (8 lengths), 400 yards (16 lengths), 500 yards (20 lengths), 1000 yards (40 lengths), 1650 yards (66 lengths). Distances for long course are: 50 meters (1 length), 100 meters (2 lengths), 200 meters (4 lengths), 400 meters (8 lengths), 800 meters (16 lengths), 1500 meters (30 lengths).

Disqualified—a swimmer's performance is not counted because of a rules infraction. A disqualification is shown by an official raising one arm with open hand above his or her head.

Diving Well—a separate pool or a pool set off to the side of the competition pool. This pool has deeper water and diving boards/platforms. During a meet, this area may be designated as a warm-down pool with proper supervision.

Dryland — the exercises and various strength programs swimmers do out of the water.

Dual Meet — type of meet where two teams/clubs compete against each other.

Electronic Timing — timing system operated on DC current (battery). The timing system usually has touchpads in the water, junction boxes on the deck with hook-up cables, buttons for backup timing, and a computer-type console that prints out the results of each race. Some systems are hooked up to a scoreboard that displays swimmers.

Entry — an individual, relay team, or club roster's event list in a swim competition.

Entry Chairperson — the host club's designated person who is responsible for receiving and making sure the entries have met the deadline.

Entry Fees — the amount per event a swimmer or relay is charged. This varies depending on the LSC and type of meet.

Event — a race or stroke over a given distance. An event equals one preliminary with its final or one timed final.

False Start — when a swimmer leaves the starting block before the horn or gun. One false start will disqualify a swimmer or a relay team, although the starter or referee may disallow the false start due to unusual circumstances.

False Start Rope — a recall rope across the width of the racing pool for the purpose of stopping swimmers who were not aware of a false start. The rope is about halfway on yard pools and about 50 feet from the starting end on meter pools.

Fastest to Slowest — a seeding method used on the longer events held at the end of a session. The fastest seeded swimmers participate in the first heats followed by the next fastest and so on.

Fees—money paid by swimmers for services (i.e,. practice fees, registration fee, USA-S membership fee, etc.).

FINA—the international rules-making organization for the sport of swimming.

Finals—the final race of each event.

Flags—pennants that are suspended over the width of each end of the pool approximately fifteen feet from the wall.

Freestyle—one of the four competitive racing strokes. Freestyle (nicknamed "free") is swum as the fourth stroke in the Medley Relay and the fourth stroke in the IM. Racing distances are 50 yards/meter, 100 yards/meter, 200 yards/meter, 400m/500yd, 800m/1000yd, 1500m/1650yd (LSCs with 8-under divisions offer the 25 yd free).

Goals—the short- and long-range targets for swimmers to aim for.

Goggles—glasses-type devices worn by swimmers to keep their eyes from being irritated by the chlorine in the water.

Gun (or Bell) Lap—the part of a freestyle distance race (400 meters or longer) when the swimmer has two lengths plus five yards to go. The starter fires a gun shot (or rings a bell) over the lane of the lead swimmer when the swimmer is at the backstroke flags.

Heats—all of the swimmers entered in the event are divided into heats, or groups of swimmers. The results are compiled by the times swam after all heats of the event are completed.

Illegal—doing something against the rules that is cause for disqualification.

IM—Individual Medley. A swimming event using all four of the competitive strokes on consecutive lengths of the race. The order must be: butterfly, backstroke, breaststroke, freestyle. Equal distances must be swum of each stroke. Distances offered: 100 yards, 200 yards/meters, 400 yards/meters.

Invitational—type of meet that requires a club to request an invitation to attend the meet.

Jump — an illegal start done by the second, third, or fourth member of a relay team. The swimmer on the block breaks contact with the block before the swimmer in the water touches the wall.

Junior Nationals — a USA-S Championship meet for swimmers eighteen years old or less. Qualification times are necessary.

Kick Board — a flotation device used by swimmers during practice.

Lane — the specific area in which a swimmer is assigned to swim (i.e, Lane 1 or Lane 2).

Lane Lines — continuous floating markers attached to a cable stretched from the starting end to the turning end for the purpose of separating each lane and quieting the waves caused by racing swimmers.

Lap — one length of the course. Sometimes may also mean down and back (2 lengths) of the course.

Leg — the part of a relay event swam by a single team member. A single stroke in the IM.

Long Course — a 50-meter pool.

LSC — local swim committee. The local level administrative division of the corporation (USA-S) with supervisory responsibilities within certain geographic boundaries designated by the corporation. There are fifty-nine LSCs.

Marshall — the official who controls the crowd and swimmer flow at a swim meet.

Meet — a series of events held in one program.

Meet Director — the official in charge of the administration of the meet. The person directing the "dry side" of the meet.

Meters — the measurement of the length of a swimming pool that was built per specs using the metric system. Long course meters is 50 meters, short course meters is 25 meters.

NAGTS — National Age Group Time Standards: the list of "C" through "AAAA" times published each year.

Nationals—USA Swimming National Championship meet conducted in March/April and August.

Natatorium—a building constructed for the purpose of housing a swimming pool and related equipment.

NCAA—National Collegiate Athletic Association.

Non-Conforming Time—a short course time submitted to qualify for a long course meet, or vice versa.

NT – No Time—the abbreviation used on a heat sheet to designate that the swimmer has not swam that event before.

Officials—the certified adult volunteers who operate the many facets of a swim competition.

Olympic Trials—the USA-S-sanctioned long course swim meet held the year of the Olympic Games to decide what swimmers will represent the USA on our Olympic team. Qualification times are faster than Senior Nationals.

Pace Clock—the electronic clocks or large clocks with highly visible numbers and second hands, positioned at the ends or sides of a swimming pool so the swimmers can read their times during warm-ups or swim practice.

Paddle—colored plastic devices worn on the swimmers hands during swim practice.

Positive Check In—the procedure required before a swimmer swims an event in a deck-seeded or pre-seeded meet. The swimmer or coach must indicate the swimmer is present and will compete.

Practice—the scheduled workouts swimmers attend with their swim team/club.

Prelims—session of a prelims/finals meet in which the qualification heats are conducted.

Prelims-Finals—type of meet with two sessions. The preliminary heats are usually held in the morning session. The fastest six or eight (Championship Heat) swimmers and the next fastest six or eight swimmers (Consolation Heat) return in the evening to compete in the finals. A swimmer who has qualified in the Consolation Finals may not place in the Championship Finals even if their finals time would place them so. The converse also applies.

Pre-seeded—a meet conducted without a bull pen in which a swimmer knows what lane and heat they are in by looking at the heat sheet or posted meet program.

Psyche Sheet—an entry sheet showing all swimmers entered into each individual event. Sometimes referred to as a "heat sheet" or meet program. However, a "heat sheet" would show not only every swimmer in an event, but also what heat and lane they are swimming in.

Pull Buoy—a flotation device used for pulling by swimmers in practice.

Qualifying Times—published times necessary to enter certain meets, or the times necessary to achieve a specific category of swimmer. See "A," "AA" (etc.) times.

Ready Room—a room poolside for the swimmers to relax before they compete in finals.

Recall Rope—a rope across the width of the racing pool for the purpose of stopping swimmers who were not aware of a false start. The rope is about half way on yard pools and about 50 feet from the starting end on meter pools.

Referee—the head official at a swim meet in charge of all of the "wet side" administration and decisions.

Relays—a swimming event in which four swimmers participate as a team. Each swimmer completes an equal distance of the race. There are two types of relays:
1) Medley relay—one swimmer swims backstroke, one swimmer swims breaststroke, one swimmer swims butterfly, one swimmer swims freestyle, in that order. Medley relays are conducted over 200 yd/m and 400 yd/m distances.
2) Freestyle relay—each swimmer swims freestyle. Free relays are conducted over 200 yd/m, 400 yd/m, and 800 yd/m distances.

Sanction—a permit issued by an LSC to a USA-S group member to conduct an event or meet.

Sanction Fee—the amount paid by a USA-S group member to an LSC for issuing a sanction.

Sanctioned Meet—a meet that is approved by the LSC in which it is held. Meet must be conducted according to USA Swimming rules. All participants, including coaches, athletes, and officials, must be USA Swimming members.

Seed—assign the swimmers heats and lanes according to their submitted or preliminary times.

Seeding—Deck Seeding: swimmers are called to report to the clerk of the course. After scratches are determined, the event is seeded. Pre-Seeding: swimmers are arranged in heats according to submitted times, usually a day prior to the meet.

Senior Meet—a meet that is for senior level swimmers and is not divided into age groups. Qualification times are usually necessary and will vary depending on the level of the meet.

Senior Nationals—a USA-S National Championship meet for swimmers of any age as long as the qualification times are met.

Session—portion of meet distinctly separated from other portions by locale, time, type of competition, or age group.

Short Course—a 25-yard or 25-meter pool.

Splash—the USA Swimming magazine that is mailed bi-monthly. A benefit of being a member of USA Swimming.

Split—a portion of an event that is shorter than the total distance and is timed (i.e., A swimmer's first 50 time is taken as the swimmer swims the 100 race). It is common to take multiple splits for the longer distances.

Start—the beginning of a race. The dive used to begin a race.

Starter—the official in charge of signaling the beginning of a race and insuring that all swimmers have a fair takeoff.

Swimming Terms – Abridged

Stand-up—the command given by the Starter or Referee to release the swimmers from their starting position.

Step-down—the command given by the Starter or Referee to have the swimmers move off the blocks. Usually this command is a good indication everything is not right for the race to start.

Stroke—there are four competitive strokes: butterfly, backstroke, breaststroke, freestyle.

Stroke Judge—the official positioned at the side of the pool, walking the length of the course as the swimmers race. If the Stroke Judge sees something illegal, they report to the referee and the swimmer may be disqualified.

Submitted Time—times used to enter swimmers in meets. These times must have been achieved by the swimmer at previous meets.

Swim-a-Thon—the "fundraiser" trademarked by USA Swimming for local clubs to use to make money.

Swim-off—in a prelims/finals-type competition, a race after the scheduled event to break a tie. The only circumstance that warrants a swim-off is to determine which swimmer makes finals or an alternate, otherwise ties stand.

Swimming World—a paid-subscription swimming magazine.

Taper—the resting phase of a swimmer at the end of the season before the championship meet.

Team Records—the statistics a team keeps, listing the fastest swimmer in the club's history for each age group/each event.

Timed Finals—competition in which only heats are swum and final placings are determined by those times.

Time Standard—a time set by a meet or LSC or USA-S (etc.) that a swimmer must achieve for qualification or recognition.

Timer—the volunteers sitting behind the starting blocks/finish end of pool, who are responsible for getting watch times on events and activating the backup buttons for the timing system.

Time Trial—an event or series of events where a swimmer may achieve or better a required time standard.

Top 10—a list of times compiled by the LSC or USA-S that recognizes the top ten swimmers in each single age group (boys and girls) by each event and distance.

Touchpad—the removable plate (on the end of pools) that is connected to an automatic timing system. A swimmer must properly touch the touchpad to register an official time in a race.

Unattached—an athlete member who competes, but does not represent a club or team (abbr. UN).

Unofficial Time—the time displayed on a read out board or read over the intercom by the announcer immediately after the race. After the time has been checked, it will become the official time.

USA-S—the governing body of swimming—USA Swimming.

USA Swimming—the national governing body of the sport headquartered in Colorado Springs.

USA-S ID Number—a sixteen-part number assigned to a swimmer after they have filled out the proper forms and paid their annual dues. The first six parts are numbers of a swimmer's birthdate: Day/Month/Year using zeros as place holders. The next three spaces are the first three letters of the athlete's legal first name. The next letter is the middle initial, followed by the first four letters of the swimmer's last name. For example: USA-S ID# for swimmer Suzanne Eileen Nelson born Aug. 27, 1976 = 082776SUZENELS.

USOTC—United States Olympic Training Center located in Colorado Springs, Colorado.

Warm-down—the recovery swimming a swimmer does after a race when pool space is available.

Warm-up—the practice and "loosening-up" session a swimmer does before the meet or his or her event is swum.

Yards—the measurement of the length of a swimming pool that was built per specs using the American system. A short course yard pool is 25 yards (75 feet) in length.

Yardage—the distance a swimmer races or swims in practice. Total yardage can be calculated for each practice session.

Bibliography

Anderson, Kelli, "Cullen Jones Seizes Swimming Spotlight," SIVault, SportsIllustrated.com, July 5, 2008, http://sportsillustrated.cnn.com/vault/article/web/COM1141691/index.htm, accessed June 6, 2012.

Donahue, Mary "History of Swimming," De Anza College, January 11, 2012. http://faculty.deanza.edu/donahuemary/Historyof swimmingsection.com, accessed June 6, 2012.

Diaz-Duran, Constantino, "The Drowning Race Gap," The Daily Beast, August 7, 2010, http://www.thedailybeast.com/articles/2010/08/07/the-louisiana-drowning-why-many-blacks-cant-swim.html, accessed June 6, 2012.

Editors, "History: How the Olympic Games Began," Reprinted with permission by the International Swimming Hall of Fame from, "Weissmuller to Spitz: The History and Background of the Olympic Game," USASwimming.org, 2010, http://www.usaswimming.org/_Rainbow/Documents/6b10d657-5680-4c23-b00f-c738870a1713/History%20of%20the%20Olympic%20Games.pdf, accessed June 6, 2012.

Editors, USA Swimming Foundation, www.usaswimming.org, accessed June 6, 2012.

Lawrence, Andrew, "Giving Kids a Lifeline," SportsIllustrated.com, August 23, 2010. http://sportsillustrated.cnn.com/vault/article/magazine/MAG1173390/index.htm, accessed June 6, 2012.

Rachel, Martin, with Wiltse, Jeff Dr., "Racial History of American Swimming Pools," National Public Radio, May 6, 2008, http://www.npr.org/templates/story/story.php?storyId=90213675, accessed June 6, 2012.

Walsh, Jeremy, "National Swimming Group Awards Five NJ Towns $400K to Teach Minority Children How to Swim," The Star Ledger, May 30, 2010. NJ.com. http://www.nj.com/news/local/index.ssf/2010/05/jersey_cities_get_money_for_sw.html, accessed June 6, 2012.

Weil, Elizabeth, "Cullen Jones, Sprinter in a Speedo," NY Times.com, July 22, 2011, http://www.nytimes.com/2011/07/24/magazine/cullen-jones-sprinter-in-a-speedo.html, accessed May 23, 2012.

Wiltse, Jeff, *Contested Waters A Social History of Swimming Pools in America* (Chapel Hill: University of North Carolina Press, 2010).

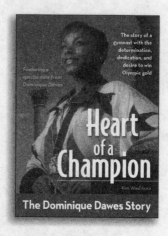

Driven by Faith:
The Trevor Bayne Story

Godwin Kelly

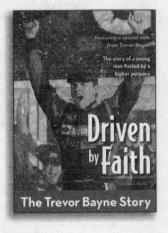

Embracing the Race. Trevor Bayne is the youngest race car driver ever to win the Daytona 500. Throughout his high-speed career, from his early start driving go-karts to his incredible win at NASCAR's biggest race, Trevor attributes all his success to God—both on and off the track. His amazing story, from start to finish, will inspire young and old, racing enthusiasts or not, as they read *Driven by Faith*, the story of a boy unafraid to share his faith, and a man who gives all the glory to God. Includes a personal note from Trevor Bayne.

Available in stores and online!

Defender of Faith: The Mike Fisher Story

Kim Washburn

Mike Fisher knows the true meaning of a power play.

As a veteran of the National Hockey League, Mike Fisher has a lot to be proud of. He plays for the Nashville Predators, was an alternate captain for the Ottawa Senators, competed in the Stanley Cup finals, and has been nominated for the Selke Trophy as the best defensive forward in the league. But it's not just his guts, grit, and talent that have brought him success. His power comes from the top—he puts his faith in Christ first and has demonstrated his love for God both on and off the ice.

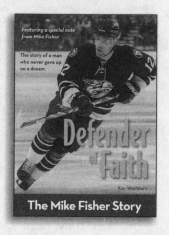

Includes a personal note from Mike Fisher.

Available in stores and online!

Gifted Hands, Kids Edition: The Ben Carson Story

Gregg Lewis & Deborah Shaw Lewis

Ben Carson used to be the class dummy. Today he is one of the world's most brilliant surgeons.

Gifted Hands, Kids Edition tells the extraordinary true story of an angry, young boy from the inner city who, through faith and determination, grew up to become one of the world's leading pediatric neurosurgeons. When Ben was in school, his peers called him the class dummy. But his mother encouraged him to succeed, and Ben discovered a deep love of learning. Ben found that anything is possible with trust and determination.

Toward the Goal:
The Kaká Story

Jeremy V. Jones

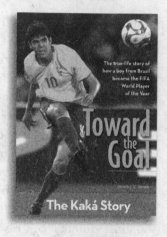

"I learned that it is faith that decides whether something will happen or not."

At the age of eight, Kaká already knew what he wanted in life: to play soccer and only soccer. He started playing in front of his friends and family, but when he suffered a crippling injury, doctors told him he would never play again. Through faith and perseverance Kaká recovered, and today he plays in front of thousands of fans every year. As the 2007 FIFA World Player of the Year and winner of the Ballon d'Or, this midfielder for Real Madrid has become one of the most recognized faces on the soccer field.

Gift of Peace: The Jimmy Carter Story

Elizabeth Raum

When Jimmy Carter was a boy, he listened to his parents talk about local politics and watched them live out their Baptist faith in the community. From the fields of his family farm to traveling the world negotiating peace talks, God guides every step of Jimmy's journey. His unwavering devotion to peace and faith helped him navigate the political waters of the governorship and presidency. Discover the extraordinary life of this world-famous humanitarian and follow in the footsteps of this incredible man of God.

Linspired, Kids Edition
The Jeremy Lin Story

Mike Yorkey and Jesse Florea

Linspired reveals the inside story of the remarkable and meteoric rise of Jeremy Lin, superstar of the New York Knicks, the first Asian-American-born player of Chinese/Taiwanese descent to play in the NBA. Discover the journey of the underdog who beat the odds to reach his current stardom and catch the attention of the sports world with both his incredible basketball skills and his

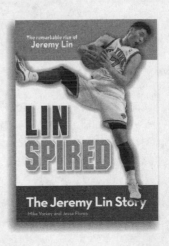

on and off-court example of faith, persistence, and hard work.

Available in stores and online!

We want to hear from you. Please send your comments about this book to us in care of zreview@zondervan.com. Thank you.